The Plot

The Will Eisner Library

The Plot

THE SECRET STORY OF
THE PROTOCOLS
OF THE ELDERS OF ZION

WILL EISNER

WITH AN INTRODUCTION BY UMBERTO ECO

W. W. NORTON & COMPANY
NEW YORK LONDON

Copyright © 2005 by the Estate of Will Eisner
Introduction copyright © 2005 by Umberto Eco

Printed in the United States of America

First Edition

For information about permission to reproduce selections from this book, write to Permissions,
W. W. Norton & Company, Inc., 500 Fifth Avenue, New York, NY 10110

Manufacturing by R. R. Donnelley, Willard Division
Production manager: Julia Druskin

Library of Congress Cataloging-in-Publication Data

Eisner, Will.
The plot : the secret story of the protocols of the Elders of Zion / by Will Eisner ; with an
introduction by Umberto Eco.
p. cm.
ISBN 0-393-06045-4
1. Protocols of the wise men of Zion. 2. Antisemitism. I. Eco, Umberto. II. Title.
DS145.P7E37 2005
305.892'4—dc22   2005040527

W. W. Norton & Company, Inc., 500 Fifth Avenue, New York, N.Y. 10110
www.wwnorton.com

W. W. Norton & Company Ltd., Castle House, 75/76 Wells Street, London W1T 3QT

1 2 3 4 5 6 7 8 9 0

Introduction

by Umberto Eco

The most extraordinary aspect of the *Protocols of the Elders of Zion* is not so much the history of its inception as that of its reception. That this fake was produced by a number of secret services and police of at least three countries, assembled from a collage of different texts, is by now a well-known fact—and Will Eisner tells it in full, taking into account the most recent research.

In one of my essays[1] I identify other sources that scholars had not taken into account: for example, the *Protocols'* "Jewish plan" for conquering the world follows, almost literally at times, the Jesuit plan as told by Eugene Sue first in *Le juif errant* (1844–45) and later in *Les mystères du people* (1849–57)—the similarities are so great that one is tempted to conclude that Maurice Joly himself (the French satirist whose pamphlet *Dialogues in Hell Between Machiavelli and Montesquieu*, published in 1864, is considered to be the direct predecessor of the *Protocols*, and who is a major figure in Eisner's *The Plot*) had been inspired by Sue's novels.

But there is more. Scholars of the *Protocols*[2] have previously reconstructed the story of Hermann Goedsche, who, in his novel *Biarritz*, written in 1868 under the pseudonym of Sir John Retcliffe, narrates how representatives of the twelve tribes of Israel gathered in the cemetery of Prague to plot the conquest of the world. Five years later, in a

---

1. "Fictional Protocols," chap. 6 in *Six Walks in the Fictional Woods* (Cambridge, Mass.: Harvard University Press, 1994).
2. See, for example, Norman Cohn, *Warrant for Genocide* (London: Eyre and Spottiswoode, 1996), chap. 1.

Russian pamphlet (*The Jews, masters of the world*), Gödsche's fictional account is related as if it had actually occurred. In 1881 *Le contemporain* reprinted the story, asserting that it originated from a reliable source— none other than British diplomat Sir John Readcliff. Then again, in 1896, François Bournand included the arguments of the Great Rabbi (who this time is called John Readclif) in his book *Les Juifs, nos contemporains*. But what no one noticed was that Gödsche had done nothing other than copy a scene from *Joseph Balsamo* (1849) by the French novelist Alexandre Dumas. In this work, Dumas recounts a meeting between Cagliostro and other Masonic conspirators in which they hatch the 1785 Diamond Necklace Affair and, with this scandal, create the right climate for the French Revolution.

This patchwork of largely fictional works makes the *Protocols* an incoherent text that easily reveals its fabricated origins. It is hardly credible, if not in a *roman feuilleton* or in a grand opera, that the "bad guys" should express their evil plans in such a frank and unashamed manner, that they should declare, as the Elders of Zion do, that they have "boundless ambition, a ravenous greed, a merciless desire for revenge and an intense hatred." If at first the *Protocols* was taken seriously, it is because it was presented as a shocking revelation, and by sources all in all trustworthy. But what seems incredible is how this fake arose from its own ashes each time someone proved that it was, beyond all doubt, a fake. This is when the "novel of the Protocols" truly starts to sound like fiction. Following the article that appeared in 1921 in the *Times* of London revealing that the *Protocols* was plagiarized, as well as every other time some authoritative source confirmed the spurious nature of the *Protocols*, there was someone else who published it again claiming its authenticity. And the story continues unabated on the Internet today. It is as if, after Copernicus, Galileo, and Kepler, one were to continue publishing textbooks claiming that the sun travels around the earth.

How can one explain resilience against all evidence, and the perverse appeal that this book continues to exercise? The answer can be found in the work of Nesta Webster, an antisemitic author who spent her life supporting this account of the Jewish plot. In her *Secret Societies and Subversive Movements*, she seems well informed and knows the whole story as Eisner narrates it here, but this is her conclusion:

The only opinion I have committed myself is that, whether genuine or not, the Protocols represent the programme of a world revolution, and that in view of their prophetic nature and of their extraordinary resemblance to the protocols of certain secret societies of the past, they were either the work of some such society or of someone profoundly versed in the lore of secret society who was able to reproduce their ideas and phraseology.[3]

Her reasoning is flawless: "since the Protocols say what I said in my story, they confirm it," or: "the Protocols confirm the story that I derived from them, and are therefore authentic." Better still: "the Protocols could be fake, but they say exactly what the Jews think, and must therefore be considered authentic." In other words, it is not the Protocols that produce antisemitism, it is people's profound need to single out an Enemy that leads them to believe in the Protocols.

I believe that—in spite of this courageous, not *comic* but *tragic* book by Will Eisner—the story is hardly over. Yet it is a story very much worth telling, for one must fight the Big Lie and the hatred it spawns.

Umberto Eco
Milan, Italy
December 2004

Translated by Alessandra Bastagli

3. Nesta Webster, *Secret Societies and Subversive Movements* (London: Boswell, 1924), pp. 408–9.

The Plot

Preface

For me, *The Plot* represents a departure from pure graphic story-telling. It marks an effort to employ this powerful medium to address a matter of immense personal concern.

My parents were Jewish-American immigrants (that, by the way, is not the only reason I remain a Jew). My father painted the interior of Catholic churches in Vienna and, when he came to America, painted scenery in the Yiddish theater in Manhattan. My parents were neither Orthodox nor Reformed, but they were "believers," which may account for my Yiddish *neshuma* (soul).

I grew up during the Great Depression and experienced prejudice—painful incidents and indignities that often befell Jews in our society at that time. I remember being angry at the shtetl attitude of my parents, who advised that we should be "quiet and not offend the goyim." To them the Holocaust was another, only much bigger, pogrom. As a student with radical inclinations in the late 1930s, I became interested in the devices that antisemites used to promote their message. There had to be some weapon other than the ancient Christian Gospels' condemnation of Jews that appeared again and again and resurrected itself, vampire-like, to reinforce antisemitism.

My search continued for nearly twenty years, but not long ago, while trolling the internet in search of frauds for a story I was contemplating, I came upon an English translation of the *Protocols of the Elders of Zion*—a document purportedly written by Jewish leaders that describes in close detail how Jews wish to conspire to take over the world—which was netcast by Radio Islam and which was also available in French,

German, Swedish, Portuguese, Russian, Spanish, and Italian. I had known about the book and had long relegated it to the library of evil literature alongside *Mein Kampf*. Only then did I actually read it and begin to probe its history.

In November of 1999, the *Washington Times* and the French weekly *L'Express* reported that research by a leading Russian historian, Mikhail Lepekhine, had unearthed evidence that the *Protocols of the Elders of Zion* was actually written in 1898 by Mathieu Golovinski, a Russian exile living in France. After five years of sifting through Russia's formerly inaccessible archives, Lepekhine came upon evidence of the *Protocols'* origin. He published his findings in *L'Express* and supposedly put to rest the question of its authorship. He corroborated a claim by the German author Konrad Heiden in 1944 that Golovinski was indeed the forger. According to *L'Express*, Lepekhine found supporting evidence in the files of Henri Bint, a Paris-based agent of the Russian policy sevices for thirty-seven years.

According to Lepekhine, here is how the story unfolded. In 1917, Sergei Svatikov, an enemy of the new revolutionary government of Russia, was engaged in dismantling the secret service of the deposed tsar. In doing so, Svatikov interrogated Bint, who told him that the author of the *Protocols* was Mathieu Golovinski, a cunning and ruthlessly ambitious youth from a tarnished aristocratic family.

In 1925, the tsar's last ambassador to France, Basil Maklakov, escaped with the Russian embassy's files and gave them to the American Hoover Foundation. Later, Svatikov defected from the new Bolshevik leadership and made off with Bint's personal files, which he had purchased from Bint. Svatikov managed to reach Prague, where he deposited the Bint files with the Russian Files Abroad, a private foundation in Prague.

After World War II, the Soviets seized the foundation and archived the files in Moscow together with State of the Federation of Russia files. Because Golovinski had become an official in the early Bolshevik movement, the Soviet Union kept a lid on these embarrassing documents. After the Communist government collapsed, Soviet files became available to researchers.

Following the first reports in *L'Express*, the influential Paris newspaper *Le Figaro* carried a major article by Victor Loupan in 2002 in which Loupan detailed Lepekhine's uncovering of the *Protocols'* authorship.

The rest of the French press apparently showed little interest in the story.

Despite such revelations, the *Protocols* has continued to gain new exposure and credibility. It is published throughout the Arab world, and in many European and Asian countries as well. For example, in June of 2003, workers of the prime minister's party in Kuala Lumpur distributed free copies of the book.

Over the years, hundreds of books and competent scholarly articles have exposed the infamy of the *Protocols*. These studies, however, are written mostly by academics and are designed to be read by scholars or by persons already convinced of their fraudulence.

I have spent my career in the application of sequential art as a form of narrative language. With the widespread acceptance of the graphic narrative as a vehicle of popular literature, there is now an opportunity to deal head-on with this propaganda in a more accessible language. It is my hope that, perhaps, this work will drive yet another nail into the coffin of this terrifying vampire-like fraud.

Tamarac, Florida
December 2004

Whenever
one group
of people
is taught
to hate
another,
a lie
is created
to
inflame
the
hatred
and justify
a
plot.

The target is easy to find

because the enemy

is always the other.

The
Original Target

In 1848, driven by a revolution in Paris, King Louis Philippe abdicated and Louis Napoleon (a nephew of Napoleon Bonaparte) was elected president of France. Four years later, after a coup d'etat, Louis Napoleon styled himself Napoleon III, emperor of France.

Napoleon III's first act as emperor was to imprison his political opponents. He was a crafty monarch, and his ambition during his reign was to seek glory through military adventurism while the great mass of French peasants remained in a state of poverty and despair.

Initially, Napoleon III achieved a short-lived public popularity by trying to "modernize" France and liberalize its economy, but his legacy remains that of a dictator and conniving politician.

In 1870, fearful that Germany was expanding too fast, Napoleon III declared war against this neighbor. The French were quickly defeated, and Napoleon III became a prisoner of war. Upon his release in 1871, he was exiled to England, where he lived until his death in 1873.

Maurice Joly

Maurice Joly was mindful of this growing tension between Germany and France. He had been born in 1821 of French parents. He was admitted to the Paris bar as an attorney and was a one-time member of the General Assembly. Joly devoted most of his time to writing caustic essays on French politics. He joined many other severe critics of Napoleon III, who regarded him as a ruthless despot.

In 1864, Joly wrote a book called "The Dialogue in Hell between Machiavelli and Montesquieu."...It intended to liken Napoleon III to the infamous Machiavelli, author of "The Prince," a treatise on the acquisition of power. Joly intended to reveal the French dictator's dark and evil plans.

1878
Paris

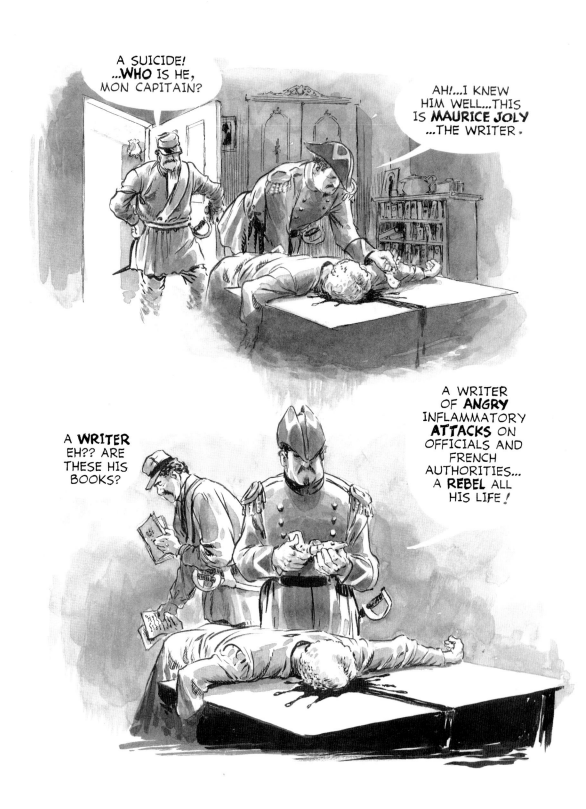

TWO MONTHS AFTER THE PUBLICATION IN BRUSSELS... COPIES OF THE BOOK BEGAN TO APPEAR IN BOOK STALLS **HERE IN PARIS...** ONCE AGAIN I WAS ASSIGNED TO **JOLY'S** CASE!

HE SERVED HIS TERM **IN PRISON.** UPON HIS RELEASE, HE JOINED THE STAFF OF A POLITICAL JOURNAL. HE QUIT THERE IN 1872 AND PUBLISHED ANOTHER BOOK, "THE HUNGRY ONES."

NOW, IN 1878, HE FILED A LAWSUIT AGAINST AN OLD COLLEAGUE M. GREVY...BUT, AS YOU SEE, HE **COMMITTED SUICIDE** BEFORE IT WAS RESOLVED!

A **SAD LIFE**...HE AND HIS WRITINGS WILL PROBABLY BE **FORGOTTEN!**

THE DIALOGUE IN HELL BETWEEN MACHIAVELLI AND MONTESQUIEU

1894
The Tsar

When Nicholas II was crowned tsar of Russia in 1894, the country was seething with unrest. Brought up by private tutors, he had little training in the affairs of state. He was dull, reactionary, and an ineffective ruler who was easily influenced.

Although revolution was slowly brewing, Russia on the surface remained a prisoner of its feudal past. In order to maintain the appearance of stability, Nicholas II engaged in a policy of suppression and later on supported pogroms against Jews.

Such antisemitic views were not new. Even before the assassination in 1881 of Alexander II (Nicholas II's grandfather) the Romanov family had been convinced of plots against the tsar.

During his own reign, Nicholas II was easily swayed by strong opinions. He veered from one plan to another depending on the advice of the most articulate in his council. His most trusted adviser was Sergei Yulievich Witte, a clever but sometimes unpopular councilor who was known to have liberal modernistic views regarded as controversial by conservatives, who dominated the court.

Witte had two very resentful enemies... GorymiKine and RachKovsKy, who were associated with the secret police.

SEE, **WITTE** HAS HIS **EAR**...BUT HOPEFULLY THE TSAR WILL **KEEP** OUR VALUES!

SURELY, HE MUST BE **AWARE** THAT RUSSIA IS FACING **A REVOLT!**

WHAT IF THERE APPEARED A DOCUMENT PROVING THAT MODERNIZATION WAS A PART OF A JEWISH PLOT?

IT WOULD BE **ABSOLUTE EVIDENCE** OF A THREAT THE **TSAR COULD NOT** IGNORE.

EXACTLY!

BRILLIANT, RACHKOVSKY! IT WILL MAKE WITTE'S ADVICE **SUSPECT!**

YES, IT WILL DAMAGE WITTE'S INFLUENCE AND IT WILL ANSWER HIS MAJESTY'S WORRY ABOUT **WHO IS BEHIND** THE UNREST! HE **DISTRUSTS** JEWS...IT'LL BE EASY...

29

BUT WHERE IS THERE SUCH A DOCUMENT? I KNOW OF NONE!

NO PROBLEM! WE WILL **MAKE** ONE IN OUR SECRET SERVICE, THE **OKHRANA BACK IN FRANCE.** WE HAVE BEEN MAKING AND **PLANTING** OUR OWN PROPAGANDA IN **THE FRENCH** PRESS FOR YEARS.

IT WILL TAKE A VERY **CUNNING** FORGER TO WRITE IT CONVINCINGLY!

WE WILL HAVE NO PROBLEM!

DON'T WORRY, GORYMIKINE...I'LL BE BACK IN MOSCOW VERY SOON WITH THE "**WEAPON.**"

30

1875
Mathieu Golovinski

Mathieu Golovinski was born in the Simbirsk region of Russia in 1865 during the reign of the Romanov dynasty. His family, a part of the fading Russian aristocracy, provided him with a fragile social standing. He grew up in a leisured environment typical of families of that class.

His father, Basil Golovinski, died, however, when Mathieu was 10 years old.

WE'VE COME AS QUICKLY AS POSSIBLE, MADAME!

WE THOUGHT IT NOT TOO SOON TO PUT YOUR PAPERS IN ORDER!

IT IS **A SAD TIME**, MADAME! YOUR HUSBAND'S DEATH AND THE TASK OF REARING A YOUNG SON.

WELL, I HAVE THE MEMORY OF A PROUD HUSBAND WHO LEFT US WITH IMPORTANT CONNECTIONS!

BASIL GOLOVINSKI WAS A CLOSE FRIEND OF **DOSTOYEVSKI**. THE GREAT AUTHOR! AND HE WAS ALSO THE SCION OF AN **ARISTOCRATIC** FAMILY! AND WE ARE RELATED TO **COUNT HENRI** OF MONS. WE'RE COMFORTABLE.

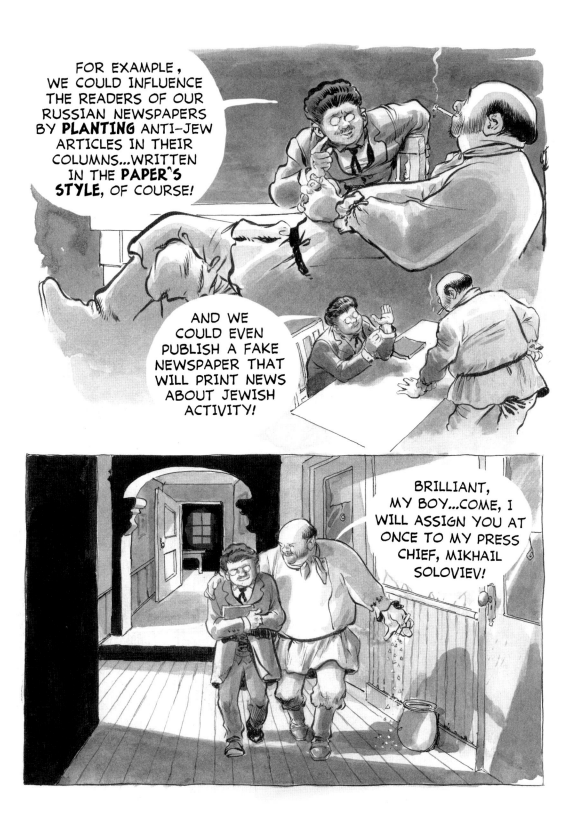

GOOD WORK! FROM HERE ON YOU WILL WRITE FOR OUR REGULAR CAMPAIGN AGAINST THE NEW MODERNIZATION!

WHY THAT?

ALL LIBERAL, CAPITALISTIC, SOCIALISTIC MOVEMENTS ARE DIRECTED BY JEWS... WE MUST EXPOSE THEM.

THEY ARE THE ANTI-CHRIST!

BUT, SIR, SHOULDN'T WE KEEP THIS POLITICAL?

IN RUSSIA RELIGION AND POLITICS ARE THE SAME!

OUR PEOPLE WILL BELIEVE ANYTHING NEGATIVE ABOUT JEWS! GO AHEAD, BOY!

I NOW APPOINT YOU MY ASSISTANT WRITER!

THANK YOU, SIR!·

49

WHAT IS THE MEANING OF THIS? **WHY** AM I ARRESTED?

1898
The Forgery

THE TSAR MUST HAVE **UNQUESTIONABLE** EVIDENCE OF A THREAT AGAINST THE MONARCHY!

IF WE COLLECT STORIES WE PLANT IN THE FRENCH PRESS...

NO!! TOO ARGUABLE... I WANT US TO UNEARTH **AN ABSOLUTELY BELIEVABLE DOCUMENT!**

BUT, RACHKOVSKY, WE ARE **ABSOLUTELY CERTAIN** THAT SUCH A DOCUMENT DOES **NOT** EXIST.

WE'LL MANUFACTURE ONE! JUST THINK HOW EXPLOSIVE THE DREYFUS AFFAIR IS.

A CLEVER **LOYAL** WRITER WE CAN TRUST PERHAPS?

AH, YES... THERE IS ONE SUCH ON OUR STAFF!

HELLO, GOLOVINSKI, HOW GOES IT WITH YOU?

NOT GOOD! I HAVE AN IMPOSSIBLE ASSIGNMENT.

LISTEN, MY FRIEND...YOU ARE A JOURNALIST... WHAT IS GOING ON WITH JEWS IN EUROPE?

WELL, IN 1897 THERE WAS THIS JEW HERZL AND HIS JEWISH NATIONAL CONGRESS.

AHH, HA! TELL ME ABOUT IT.

WELL, THEY HAD A MEETING IN BASEL! A LOT OF JEWS FROM ALL OVER CAME LAST YEAR.

YES, YES, GO ON...DID THEY ISSUE A MANIFESTO? A PLAN TO RISE UP AGAINST US...

NO, THEY JUST WANT A JEWISH NATIONAL STATE.

NO CONSPIRACY?

NO...

1905
Russia
The First Publication

 IT IS A PROGRAM OF **JEWISH WORLD CONQUEST**...PROOF OF WHO IS BEHIND THIS REVOLUTION!

HMM!

IT MUST BE SHOWN TO THE TSAR **AT ONCE.** ...**REBELLION** IS FILLED WITH **JEWISH INFLUENCE.**

 WHERE DID YOU GET THE DOCUMENT, NILUS?

IT WAS GIVEN TO ME BY **SUKHOTIN,** WHO SECURED IT FROM OUR **OKHRANA** IN PARIS...BEYOND THAT I CANNOT TELL YOU!

YES INDEED. ...THIS WILL BE OF **GREAT INTEREST** TO THE **TSAR.**

 THE SANCTITY OF OUR MONARCHY IS THE WILL OF GOD... CHRISTIANS MUST DEFEND IT!

 GET HIM OUT OF HERE!

1905

Tsar Nicholas II made inept efforts to mollify his angry people by granting basic liberties and allowing a parliament (Duma), which he kept dissolving. Meanwhile he ruthlessly suppressed the people's risings. Royal troops fired on a peaceful march of workers in St. Petersburg on January 9, known as Bloody Sunday. Anti-Jewish pogroms were rampant. The Russian edition, published by Dr. Nilus, of the "Protocols of Zion" was widely circulated. Monarchists frequently read it aloud to illiterate peasants.

1914

The start of World War I led to Russian military defeats. A failing economy brought about terrible civilian suffering. Loyalists openly spoke about a "Jewish plot."

1917

Food riots, strikes, and the tsar's panicky dissolution of the Fourth Duma exploded into revolution. By November, the Bolsheviks (the revolutionary faction of the former Social Democratic workers' party) had seized control of the government. Royalist Russians began a civil war and were defeated. Tsar Nicholas II abdicated and was executed, along with his family, by Bolsheviks in 1918.

Russian aristocrats fled Russia and dispersed throughout Europe, the Far East, and the Middle East. There they settled as expatriates. Most had little work experience. In order to earn money, they frequently sold valuables. Some of these items provided information on the Russian use of antisemitic literature.

1920

The Times

LONDON, SATURDAY, MAY 8, 1920.

"THE JEWISH PERIL."

A DISTURBING PAMPHLET

CALL FOR INQUIRY.

(FROM A CORRESPONDENT.)

The Times has not as yet noticed this singular little book. Its diffusion is, however, increasing, and its reading is likely to perturb the thinking public. Never before have a race and a creed been accused of a more sinister conspiracy. We in this country, who live in good fellowship with numerous representatives of Jewry, may well ask that some authoritative criticism should deal with it, and either destroy the ugly "Semitic" bogy or assign their proper place to the insidious allegations of this kind of literature.

In spite of the urgency of impartial and exhaustive criticism, the pamphlet has been allowed, so far, to pass almost unchallenged. The Jewish Press announced, it is true, that the anti-Semitism of the "Jewish Peril" was going to be exposed. But save for an unsatisfactory article in the March 5 issue of the *Jewish Guardian* and for an almost equally unsatisfactory contribution to the *Nation* of March 27, this exposure is yet to come. The article of the *Jewish Guardian* is unsatisfactory, because it deals mainly with the personality of the author of the book in which the pamphlet is embodied, with Russian reactionary propaganda, and the Russian secret police. It does not touch the substance of the "Protocols of the Learned Elders of Zion." The purely Russian side of the book and its fervid "Orthodoxy" is not its most interesting feature. Its author—Professor S. Nilus—who was a minor official in the Department of Foreign Religions at Moscow, had, in all likelihood, opportunities of access to many archives and unpublished documents. On the other hand, the world-wide issue raised by the "Protocols" which he incorporated in his book and are now translated into English as "The Jewish Peril," cannot fail not only to interest, but to preoccupy. What are the theses of the "Protocols" with which, in the absence of public criticism, British readers have to grapple alone and unaided? They are, ~~~hly :—~~~

dominion only to find beneath it another more dangerous because more secret? Have we, by straining every fibre of our national body, escaped a "Pax Germanica" only to fall into a "Pax Judæica"? The "Elders of Zion," as represented in their "Protocols" are by no means kinder taskmasters than William II. and his henchmen would have been. All these questions, which are likely to obtrude themselves on the reader of the "Jewish Peril" cannot be dismissed by a shrug of the shoulders unless one wants to strengthen the hand of the typical anti-Semite and call forth his favourite accusation of the "conspiracy of silence." An impartial investigation of these would-be documents and of their history is most desirable. That history is by no means clear from the English translation. They would appear, from internal evidence, to have been written by Jews for Jews, or to be cast in the form of lectures, and notes for lectures, by Jews to Jews. If so, in what circumstances were they produced and to cope with what inter-Jewish emergency? Or are we to dismiss the whole matter without inquiry and to let the influence of such a book as this work unchecked?

ZIONIST ASPIRATIONS.

DR. WEIZMANN ON FUTURE OF PALESTINE.

Dr. Weizmann, the Zionist leader, who has just returned from the Conference at San Remo, in the course of a statement yesterday on the future of Palestine expressed his appreciation, and that of his fellow Zionists, for the assistance rendered to their cause by *The Times*. The Balfour declaration, by being incorporated in the Treaty with Turkey, had received international sanction. Dealing with the mandate conferred on Great Britain, he said:—

There are still important details outstanding, such as the actual terms of the mandate and the question of boundaries in Palestine. There is the delimitation of the boundary between French Syria and Palestine, which will constitute the northern frontier and the eastern line of demarcation, adjoining Arab Syria. The latter is not likely to be fixed until the Emir Feisal attends the Peace Conference, probably in Paris.

I must clear up a misapprehension (he continued). Palestine is not going to be a purely Jewish State; it is going to be controlled by a British Administration for some time, with the object held steadily in view of making it a Jewish national home in the future. The first aims will be to ~~~~~~~~~~

1921
Constantinople

SET THEM SIDE BY SIDE, GRAVES, AND YOU WILL SEE **OBVIOUS PLAGIARISM** OF JOLY'S "DIALOGUE"!

I SEE...BE PATIENT WHILE I GO THROUGH IT...YES! YES! YES!

DIALOGUE IN HELL

FIRST DIALOGUE

Machiavelli: The evil instinct in man is more powerful than the good. Man leans more toward the evil than the good; fear and power have more control over him than reason.... All men seek power, and there is none who would not be an oppressor if he could; all, or nearly all, are ready to sacrifice the rights of others to their own interests.

What restrains these ravenous animals that we call men? In the beginnings of society, it is brute force, without control; later, it is the law, that is, force again, ruled by certain forms. You have consulted all the sources of history; everywhere force appears before justice.

Political liberty is only a relative idea....

PROTOCOLS

NUMBER 1, paras. 3-6

It must be noted that men with bad instincts are more in number than the good, and therefore the best results in governing them are attained by violence and terrorization, and not by academic discussions. Every man aims at power, everyone would like to become a dictator if only he could, and rare indeed are the men who would not be willing to sacrifice the welfare of all for the sake of securing their own welfare. What has restrained the beasts of prey who are called men? What has served for their guidance hitherto?

In the beginnings of the structure of society they were subjected to brute and blind force: afterwards to law, which is the same force, only disguised. I draw the conclusion that by the law of nature right lies in force. Political freedom is an idea but not a fact.

DIALOGUE IN HELL

FIRST DIALOGUE

States, once constituted, have two kinds of enemies: the enemies within and the enemies without. What arms shall they employ in war against the foreigners? Will the two enemy generals communicate to one another their campaign plans in order that each shall be able to defend himself? Will they forbid themselves night attacks, snares, ambuscades, battles in which the number of troops are unequal? Without doubt, they will not. And such fighters would make one laugh. And these snares, these artifices, all this strategy indispensable to warfare, you don't want them to be employed against the enemies within, against the disturbers of peace?... Is it possible to conduct by pure reason violent masses which are moved only by sentiment, passion, and prejudice?

PROTOCOLS

NUMBER 1, paras. 9, 10

If every State has two foes, and if in regard to the external foe it is allowed and not considered immoral to use every manner and art of conflict, as for example to keep the enemy in ignorance of plans of attack and defense, to attack him by night or in superior numbers, then in what way can the same means in regard to a worse foe, the destroyer of the structure of society and the commonweal, be called immoral and not permissible?

Is it possible for any sound logical mind to hope with any success to guide crowds by the aid of reasonable counsels and arguments, when any objection or contradiction, senseless though it may be, can be made and when such objection may find more favor with the people, whose powers of reasoning are superficial?

THE BASIC IDEAS ARE THE **SAME** DESPITE WORD CHANGES LIKE... "two kinds of enemies" **VERSUS** "two foes."

DIALOGUE IN HELL

FIRST DIALOGUE

Machiavelli: Has politics anything to do with morals?…

This word "justice" itself, by the way, do you not see that it is infinitely vague?

Where does it begin, where does it end? When will justice exist, when will it not exist? I take examples. Here is a State: bad organization of public powers, turbulence of democracy, impotence of laws to control discontented disorder, which reins everywhere, will all precipitate it into ruin. A strong man thrusts himself from the ranks of the aristocracy or from the heart of the people; he breaks through all constituted power; he puts his hand on the laws, he alters all the institutions, and he gives twenty years of peace to his country. Did he have the right to do what he has done?

PROTOCOLS

NUMBER 1, paras. 11,12,13,14

The political has nothing in common with the moral.

The word "right" is an abstract thought and proved by nothing.

Where does right begin? Where does it end?

In any State in which there is a bad organization of authority, an impersonality of laws and of the rights over multiplying out of liberalism, I find a new right to attack by the right of the strong, and to scatter to the winds all existing forces of order and regulation, to reconstruct all institutions and to become sovereign lord of those who have left to us the rights of their power by laying them down voluntarily in their liberalism.

THE "PROTOCOLS" WRITTEN **IN 1897** STATES THAT THE ELDERS DECREED THE EXPULSION OF ALL NON-JEWISH SECRET SOCITIES!

I QUESTION THAT! FOR IN **1851** NAPOLEON III, JOLY'S ENEMY, BANNED AND IMPRISONED 26,000 MEMBERS OF SECRET SOCIETIES IN FRANCE **...46 YEARS BEFORE** THE "PROTOCOLS"!

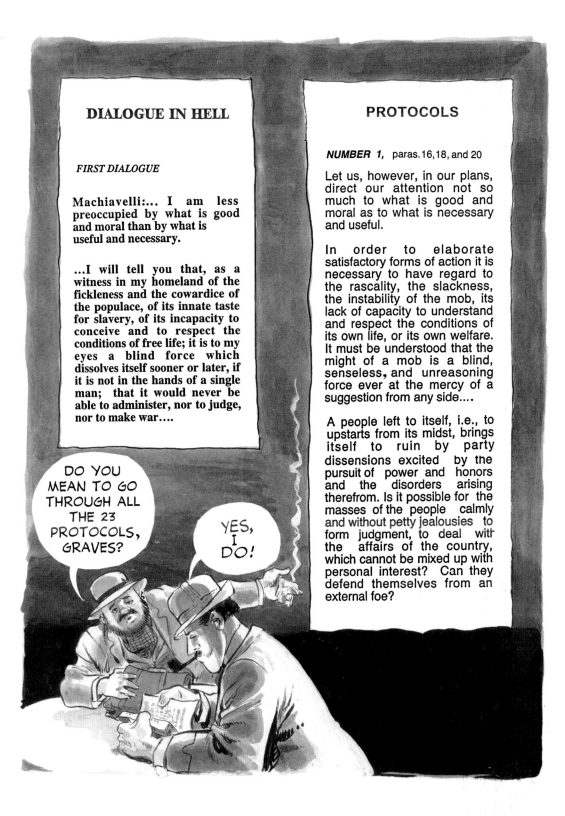

DIALOGUE IN HELL

FIRST DIALOGUE

Machiavelli:... I am less preoccupied by what is good and moral than by what is useful and necessary.

...I will tell you that, as a witness in my homeland of the fickleness and the cowardice of the populace, of its innate taste for slavery, of its incapacity to conceive and to respect the conditions of free life; it is to my eyes a blind force which dissolves itself sooner or later, if it is not in the hands of a single man; that it would never be able to administer, nor to judge, nor to make war....

PROTOCOLS

NUMBER 1, paras.16,18, and 20

Let us, however, in our plans, direct our attention not so much to what is good and moral as to what is necessary and useful.

In order to elaborate satisfactory forms of action it is necessary to have regard to the rascality, the slackness, the instability of the mob, its lack of capacity to understand and respect the conditions of its own life, or its own welfare. It must be understood that the might of a mob is a blind, senseless, and unreasoning force ever at the mercy of a suggestion from any side....

A people left to itself, i.e., to upstarts from its midst, brings itself to ruin by party dissensions excited by the pursuit of power and honors and the disorders arising therefrom. Is it possible for the masses of the people calmly and without petty jealousies to form judgment, to deal with the affairs of the country, which cannot be mixed up with personal interest? Can they defend themselves from an external foe?

DO YOU MEAN TO GO THROUGH ALL THE 23 PROTOCOLS, GRAVES?

YES, I DO!

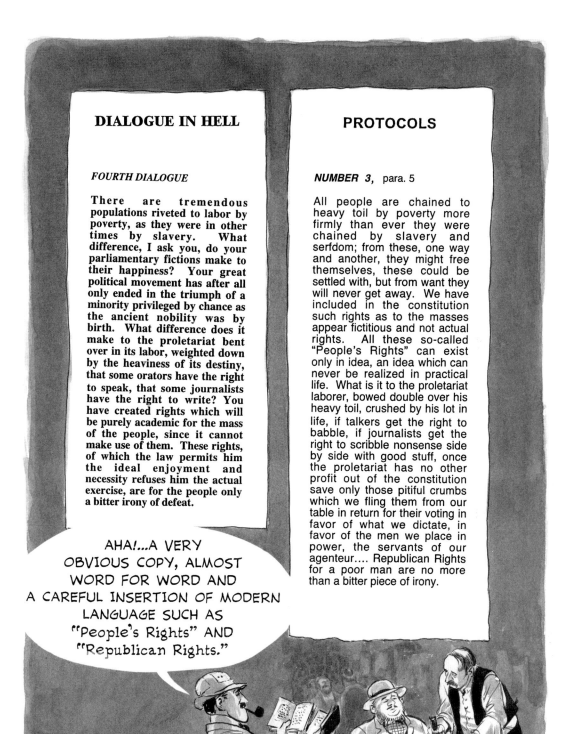

DIALOGUE IN HELL

FOURTH DIALOGUE

There are tremendous populations riveted to labor by poverty, as they were in other times by slavery. What difference, I ask you, do your parliamentary fictions make to their happiness? Your great political movement has after all only ended in the triumph of a minority privileged by chance as the ancient nobility was by birth. What difference does it make to the proletariat bent over in its labor, weighted down by the heaviness of its destiny, that some orators have the right to speak, that some journalists have the right to write? You have created rights which will be purely academic for the mass of the people, since it cannot make use of them. These rights, of which the law permits him the ideal enjoyment and necessity refuses him the actual exercise, are for the people only a bitter irony of defeat.

PROTOCOLS

NUMBER 3, para. 5

All people are chained to heavy toil by poverty more firmly than ever they were chained by slavery and serfdom; from these, one way and another, they might free themselves, these could be settled with, but from want they will never get away. We have included in the constitution such rights as to the masses appear fictitious and not actual rights. All these so-called "People's Rights" can exist only in idea, an idea which can never be realized in practical life. What is it to the proletariat laborer, bowed double over his heavy toil, crushed by his lot in life, if talkers get the right to babble, if journalists get the right to scribble nonsense side by side with good stuff, once the proletariat has no other profit out of the constitution save only those pitiful crumbs which we fling them from our table in return for their voting in favor of what we dictate, in favor of the men we place in power, the servants of our agenteur.... Republican Rights for a poor man are no more than a bitter piece of irony.

AHA!...A VERY OBVIOUS COPY, ALMOST WORD FOR WORD AND A CAREFUL INSERTION OF MODERN LANGUAGE SUCH AS "People's Rights" AND "Republican Rights."

DIALOGUE IN HELL

FOURTH DIALOGUE

Machiavelli: You do not know the unfathomable cowardice of humanity, servile in the face of force, pitiless in the face of weakness, implacable before blunders, indulgent before crimes, incapable of supporting the contrarieties of a liberal regime, and patient to the point of martyrdom before all the violences of bold despotism, upsetting thrones in its moments of anger, and giving itself rulers whom it pardons for actions the least of which would have caused it to decapitate twenty constitutional kings.

PROTOCOLS

NUMBER 3,   para. 16

It is the bottomless rascality of the *goyim* peoples, who crawl on their bellies to force, but are merciless toward weakness, unsparing to faults, and indulgent to crimes, unwilling to bear the contradictions of a free social system but patient unto martyrdom under the violence of a bold despotism. It is those qualities which are aiding us to independence. From the premier-dictators of the present day the *goyim* peoples suffer patiently and bear such abuse as for the least of them they would have beheaded twenty kings.

AN OBVIOUS INEPTITUDE!...NOTICE "Humanity" IN THE "DIALOGUE" BECOMES "Goyim" IN THE "PROTOCOLS," A YIDDISH WORD TAKEN FROM THE HEBREW THAT JEWS USE FOR GENTILES. COULD ANYONE BELIEVE THAT THE ELDERS WOULD BE SO NAIVE AND CARELESS AS TO EMPLOY **A COMMON ETHNIC** WORD IN SUCH A FORMAL TRACT AS THE "PROTOCOLS"?

DIALOGUE IN HELL

NINTH DIALOGUE

Machiavelli: And where have you ever seen that a constitution, really worthy of the name, really durable, has ever been the result of popular deliberation? A constitution must come forth fully armed from the head of one man alone, or it is nothing but a work condemned to oblivion. Without homogeneity, without linking of parties, without practical strength, it will necessarily bear the imprint of all the weaknesses of sight that have presided at its composition....

Montesquieu: ...One would say, to hear you, that you are going to draw a people out of chaos or out of the deep night of their first origins....

Machiavelli: I do not say no; therefore you will see that I need not destroy your institutions from top to bottom to arrive at my goal. It will suffice me to modify the arrangements and to change the methods.

PROTOCOLS

NUMBER 10, paras. 6,7

A scheme of government should come ready made from one brain, because it will never be clinched firmly if it is allowed to split into fractional parts in the minds of many. It is allowable, therefore, for us to have cognizance of the scheme of action but not to discuss it lest we disturb its artfulness, the interdependence of its component parts, the practical force of the secret meaning of each clause. To discuss and make alteration in a labor of this kind by means of numerous votings is to impress upon it the stamp of all ratiocinations and misunderstandings which have failed to penetrate the depth and nexus of its plottings....

These schemes will not turn existing institutions upside down just yet. They will only effect changes in their economy and consequently in the whole combined movement of their progress, which will thus be directed along the paths laid down in our schemes.

HERE WE CAN CLEARLY SEE HOW AN IDEA IS COPIED!

DIALOGUE IN HELL

TENTH DIALOGUE

Machiavelli:...Now, once more, what is the Council of State? ...It is nothing but a Draughting Committee. When the Council of State makes a law, it is really the sovereign who makes it; when it renders a judgment, it is the sovereign who renders it....

Montesquieu: It is true that if we evaluate the sum of the powers which lie in your hands, you ought to begin to be satisfied.

To sum up:

You make the laws: 1. in the form of propositions to the legislative body; 2. in the form of decrees; 3. in the form of senatorial decrees; 4. in the form of general regulations; 5. in the form of resolutions at the Council of State; 6. in the form of ministerial regulations; 7. and, finally, in the form of coups d'état.

PROTOCOLS

NUMBER 11, paras. 1,2

The State Council has been, as it were, the emphatic expression of the ruler; it will be, as the "show" part of the Legislative Corps, what may be called the editorial committee of the laws and decrees of the ruler.

This, then, is the program of the new constitution. We shall make Law, Right, and Justice (1) in the guise of proposals to the Legislative Corps, (2) by decrees of the president under the guise of general regulations, of orders of the Senate and of resolutions of the State Council in the guise of ministerial orders, (3) and in case a suitable occasion should arise, in the form of a revolution in the State.

WHEN COPYING THE "DIALOGUES"... WHY WOULD THE "PROTOCOLS" ALTER "coups d'état" TO "revolution"?

OBVIOUSLY IT WAS TO ADDRESS THE TSAR'S CONCERN OVER A RUSSIAN REVOLUTION, EH?

DIALOGUE IN HELL

THIRTEENTH DIALOGUE

Machiavelli: This is because you do not understand, Montesquieu! How much impotence and even simplicity is found among the majority of men of European demagoguism. These tigers have souls of sheep, heads full of wind. Their dream is the absorption of the individual into a symbolic unity. They demand the complete realization of equality.

PROTOCOLS

NUMBER 15, para. 6

You cannot imagine to what extent the wisest of the Goyim can be brought to a state of unconscious naiveté in the presence of this condition of high conceit of themselves, and at the same time how easy it is to take the heart out of them.... These tigers in appearance have the souls of sheep and the wind blows freely through their heads. We have set them on the hobby-horse of an idea about the absorption of individuality by the symbolic unit of Collectivism....

"...Tigers with the souls of sheep and heads full of wind..." A CLEVER METAPHOR...NO WONDER THE "PROTOCOLS" COPIES IT!

DIALOGUE IN HELL

SEVENTEENTH DIALOGUE

Montesquieu:... Now I understand the apologue the god Vishnu; you have a hundred arms like the Hindu idol and each one of your fingers touches a spring. In the same way that you touch everything, are you also able to see everything?

Machiavelli: Yes, for I shall make of the police an institution so vast that in the heart of my kingdom half of the people shall see the other half....

...If, as I scarcely doubt, I succeed in attaining this result, here are some of the forms by which my police would manifest themselves abroad: men of pleasure and good company in the foreign courts, to keep an eye on the intrigues of the princes and of the exiled pretenders...the establishment of political newspapers in the great capitals, printers and book stores placed in the same conditions and secretly subsidized....

PROTOCOLS

NUMBER 17, paras. 7,8

Our kingdom will be an apologia of the divinity Vishnu, in whom is found its personification – in our hundred hands will be, one in each, the springs of the machinery of social life. We shall see everything without the aid of official police.... In our programs one-third of our subjects will keep the rest under observation....

Our agents will be taken from the higher as well as the lower ranks of society, from among the administrative class who spend their time in amusements, editors, printers, and publishers, booksellers, clerks, and salesmen, workmen, coachmen, lackeys, et cetera....

DIALOGUE IN HELL

TWENTIETH DIALOGUE

Montesquieu: After all, the expenditures must be in proportion to the revenues....

Machiavelli: Now, this is how things work out: the general budget, the one which is voted at the beginning of the year, comes to a total amount of, let us say, 800 millions. When half of the year is gone, the financial facts already no longer correspond to the first estimates; so what is called a rectifying budget is presented in the Chambers, and this budget adds 100 millions, 150 millions to the original figure. Then comes the supplementary budget: it adds 50 or 60 millions;

PROTOCOLS

NUMBER 20,   paras. 26-32

The budgets of income and expenditure will be carried out side by side that they may not be obscured by distance one to another.

...The first irregularity, as we shall point out, consists in their beginning with drawing up a single budget which year after year grows owing to the following cause: this budget is dragged out to half the year, then they demand a

Continued

CLEARLY, THE "PROTOCOLS" AUTHOR ADAPTS THE TEXT OF "DIALOGUES" SO CARELESSLY IN HIS HASTY ATTEMPT TO **PROVE** A JEWISH CONSPIRACY!

DIALOGUE IN HELL

finally comes the liquidation which adds 15, 20, or 30 millions. In short, in the general reckoning, the total of the unforeseen expenses forms one-third of the estimated expenditures. It is upon this last figure that the legislative vote of the Chambers falls as a form of confirmation. In this way, at the end of ten years the budget can be doubled and even tripled....

Montesquieu:... It is certain that there are few governments who are not obliged to have recourse to borrowing; but it is also certain that they are obliged to make use of them sparingly; they could not, without immorality and danger, encumber future generations with exorbitant burdens, out of all proportion to

PROTOCOLS

supplementary budget, and all this ends up in accordance with the sum of the total addition, the annual departure from the normal reaches up as much as 50 percent in a year, and so the annual budget is trebled in ten years....

Every kind of loan proves infirmity in the State and a want of understanding of the rights of the State. Loans hang like a sword of Damocles over the heads of rulers, who, instead of taking from their subjects by a temporary tax, come begging with outstretched palm of our bankers...the Goy states go on in persisting in putting more on to themselves so that they must inevitably perish, drained by voluntary blood-letting.

THEIR INTEREST CALCULATIONS ARE THE **SAME** TO SUPPORT THE FINANCIAL DANGERS OF LOANS!

DIALOGUE IN HELL

probable resources. How are loans made? By the issue of bonds containing an obligation on the part of the government to pay a yearly interest proportionate to the capital which has been deposited. If the loan is at 5 percent, for instance, the state, at the end of twenty years, has paid a sum equal to the capital borrowed; at the end of forty years, a double amount; at the end of sixty years, a triple amount, and yet it always remains debtor for the total of the same capital. The modern states wished to put a necessary

PROTOCOLS

What also indeed is, in substance, a loan, especially a foreign loan? A loan is an issue of government bills of exchange containing a percentage obligation commensurate to the sum of the loan capital. If the loan bears a charge of 5 percent, then in twenty years the State vainly pays away in interest a sum equal to the loan borrowed, in forty years it is paying a souble sum, in sixty treble, and all the while the debt remains an unpaid debt.

From this calculation it is obvious that with any form of taxation per head the State is bailing out the last coppers of the poor taxpayers in order to settle accounts...instead of collecting

THESE TWO BOOKS WERE WRITTEN **40 YEARS** APART FROM EACH OTHER ...WHY IS THE **SAME** INTEREST RATE EMPLOYED BY THE "PROTOCOLS"? SURELY THEY MUST HAVE CHANGED DURING ALL THAT TIME.

VERY REVEALING ...EH?

DIALOGUE IN HELL

limitation to the increase of taxes. So they conceived a scheme truly admirable for its simplicity.... A special fund was created, the capitalized resources of which are meant to be a permanent redemption of the public debt by successive fractions; so that every time the state borrows, it must endow the sinking fund with a certain capital for the purpose of liquidating the new debt at a given time....

Our system of accounting, fruit of long experience, is distinguished by the clarity and the certitude of its procedures. It obstructs abuses and gives to no one, from the smallest official to the chief of state himself, the means of diverting the least sum from its original purpose, or of making irregular use of it.

PROTOCOLS

these coppers for its own need without additional interest.

So long as loans were internal the Goyim only shuffled their money from the pockets of the poor to those of the rich, but when we brought up the necessary person in order to transfer the loans into the external sphere, all the wealth of States flowed into our cashboxes....

We shall so hedge about our system of accounting that neither the ruler nor the most insignificant public servant will be in a position to divert even the smallest sum from its destination without detection or to direct it in another direction except that which will be once fixed in a definite plan of action.

NOW...**WHY** WOULD THE ELDERS OF ZION IN THEIR PROTOCOLS OF WORLD DOMINATION DEVOTE SO MUCH TIME TO THE **MUNDANE** DETAILS OF FINANCIAL MANAGEMENT??

DIALOGUE IN HELL

TWENTY-FIRST DIALOGUE

Machiavelli: I am afraid that you are somewhat prejudiced against loans;... modern economists today expressly recognize that, far from impoverishing the state, public debts enrich it. Will you allow me to explan how?

Montesquieu:...I should first of all like to know from whom you will ask so much capital, and for what reason you will ask it.

Machiavelli: For that, foreign wars are a great help. In the great states, they permit the borrowing of five or six hundred millions; one manages so as to spend only the half or two-thirds, and the rest finds its place in the treasury for domestic expenditures.

PROTOCOLS

NUMBER 21, paras. 1, 11

To what I reported to you at the last meeting I shall say nothing more, because they have fed us with national moneys of the Goyim....

We have taken advantage of the venality of administrators and slackness of rulers to get our moneys twice, thrice, and more times over, by lending to Goy governments moneys which were not .

...UNLESS, OF COURSE, THIS WAS **NOT WRITTEN BY THE ELDERS** AT ALL... AS WE SUSPECT!

DIALOGUE IN HELL

TWENTY-THIRD THROUGH TWENTY-FIFTH DIALOGUES

Machiavelli:...The cult of the prince is a sort of religion and, like all possible religions, this cult prescribes contradictions and mysteries beyond reason.

...I wish my aims to be impenetrable, even to those who are closest to me. I would only communicate my projects when I gave the command for execution....

His counselors ask one another secretly what he will think of next. He personifies in their eyes the Providence whose ways are

PROTOCOLS

NUMBER 24, paras. 3-15

Certain members of the seed of David will prepare the kings and their heirs inducting them into the most secret mysteries of the political, into schemes of government, but providing always that none may come to knowledge of the secrets....

The king's plan of action for the current moment, and all the more so for the future, will be unknown, even to those who are called his closest counselors.

Only the king and the three who stood sponsor for him will know what is coming.

In the person of the king who with unbending will is master...

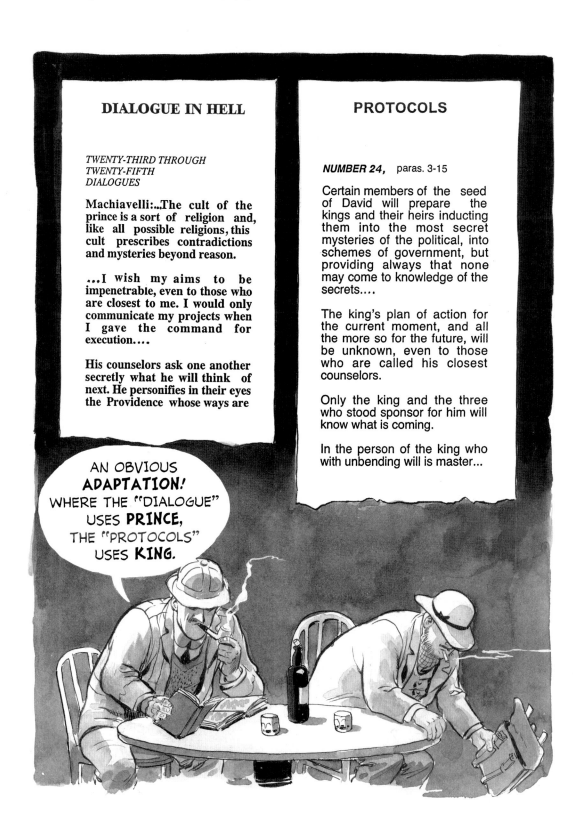

DIALOGUE IN HELL

inscrutable....They never know if some enterprise already prepared will not descend on them from one day to the other.

A Prince whose power is founded upon a democratic base, must speak carefully, albeit popularly. If necessary he must not fear to speak like a demagogue, for after all he is the people, and he must have its passions....

You asked me a moment ago if I knew self-denial, if I would sacrifice myself for my people, relinquish the throne if necessary; now you have my answer, I can relinquish it as a martyr.

PROTOCOLS

of himself and of humanity all will discern as it were fate with its mysterious ways. None will know what the king wishes to attain by his dispositions, and therefore none will dare to stand across an unknown path....

That the people may know and love their king, it is indispensable for him to converse in the market-places with his people. This ensures the necessary clinching of two forces which are now divided one from another by us by the terror.

The prop of humanity in the person of the supreme lord of all the world of the holy seed of David must sacrifice to his people all personal inclinations.

89

WELL?? YOU'VE COMPARED THEM...ER... HOW MUCH WILL "THE TIMES" **PAY**? ...I'LL GIVE YOU MY ADDRESS!

YES, **IF** THEY BUY IT...THE PRICE WILL HAVE TO BE **NEGOTIATED**...YOU UNDERSTAND?

IF THE "PROTOCOLS" IS INDEED A **FRAUD**, OUR RESEARCHERS WILL **PROVE** IT AND EXPOSE THE FAKE!

IF THESE GENEVA DIALOGUES ARE VALID "THE TIMES" WILL PUT IT RIGHT.

SIR??? EH! **GONE!** NOT TO WORRY. HE'LL BE BACK TO **COLLECT!**

TELEGRAF

1921

The Times

LONDON, WEDNESDAY, AUGUST 17, 1921.

"JEWISH PERIL" EXPOSED.

HISTORIC "FAKE."

DETAILS OF THE FORGERY.

MORE PARALLELS.

We published yesterday an article from our Constantinople Correspondent, which showed that the notorious "Protocols of the Elders of Zion"— one of the mysteries of politics since 1905—were a clumsy forgery, the text being based on a book published in French in 1865.

The book, without title page, was obtained by our Correspondent from a Russian source, and we were able to identify it with a complete copy in the British Museum.

The disclosure, which naturally aroused the greatest interest among those familiar with Jewish questions, finally disposes of the "Protocols" as credible evidence of a Jewish plot against civilization.

We publish below a second article, which gives further close parallels between the language of the Protocols and that attributed to Machiavelli and Montesquieu in the volume dated from Geneva.

PLAGIARISM AT WORK.
(From Our Constantinople Correspondent.)

While the Geneva Dialogues open with an exchange of compliments between Montesquieu and Machiavelli, which covers seven pages, the author of the Protocols plunges at once *in medias res.*

One can imagine him hastily turning over those first seven pages of the book which he has been ordered to paraphrase against time, and angrily ejaculating, "Nothing here." But on page 8 of the Dialogues he finds what he wants;

GOOD WORK GRAVES...WE FINALLY **PAID** YOUR EMIGRE £300 FOR IT...NOW IF WE CAN **FIND** GOLOVINSKI AND GET HIS CONFESSION...

HAH!...HE JOINED THE BOLSHEVIKS.

GOLOVINSKI BECAME A PARTY **ACTIVIST** AND ROSE TO BE AN ADVISER TO TROTSKY. BUT HE **DIED** LAST YEAR!

WELL, THAT'S THAT!

OH BUT GRAVES, "THE TIMES" IS INFLUENTIAL... AFTER OUR **EXPOSÉ** WE'LL PROBABLY HEAR NO MORE OF THIS FRAUD!

I'M NOT SO SURE!

ANTI-BOLSHEVIKS, **WHITE RUSSIANS**, PUBLISHED THOUSANDS OF COPIES! HERE'S A PAGE FROM NILUS'S "THE GREAT IN THE SMALL."

1921
Germany

1923
Germany

1926

Adolf Hitler, while spending three years in jail for the **BEER HALL PUTSCH,** writes his famous book *"MEIN KAMPF."*

To what extent the whole existence of this [Jewish] people is based on a continuous lie is shown incomparably by THE PROTOCOLS OF THE ELDERS OF ZION.

The important g is that with ively terrifying nty they reveal e true nature and activity of the Jewish people and expose their inner contexts as well as their final aims.

1933
Bern, Switzerland

The Reichstag Fire plotted by Adolf Hitler's followers brought him to power in Germany. The Nazis quickly attempted to export their ideas to the rest of Europe.

1934
Bern, Switzerland
The Trial

April 1935

SINCE ITS FIRST PUBLICATION IN RUSSIA BY DR. NILUS IN 1905, **FOUR PRINTINGS HAVE BEEN DISTRIBUTED THERE!**

IN 1919, TYPE-SCRIPT COPIES WERE DISTRIBUTED TO DELEGATES AT THE VERSAILLES PEACE CONFERENCE BY WHITE RUSSIANS.

IN ENGLAND **VICTOR MARSDEN** TRANSLATED THE "PROTOCOLS" INTO ENGLISH IN 1922.

IN 1920, **THE FIRST POLISH LANGUAGE EDITION** WAS BROUGHT INTO THE UNITED STATES AND SOUTH AMERICA BY POLISH IMMIGRANTS.

IN 1921, THE **FIRST ARABIC** AND THE **FIRST ITALIAN** COPIES APPEARED!

IN 1921, "THE TIMES" OF LONDON PUBLISHED ITS FAMOUS **EXPOSÉ** OF THIS **FALSE** DOCUMENT!

AND BECAUSE OF HIS FAME, **HENRY FORD'S** WORK DESERVES RECOUNTING!

IN 1920, HENRY FORD THE AMERICAN AUTO MAGNATE, BOUGHT A SMALL NEWSPAPER, THE "DEARBORN INDEPENDENT." HE BEGAN A SERIES, "THE INTERNATIONAL JEW," MADE UP OF BORROWINGS FROM THE "PROTOCOLS OF THE ELDERS ON ZION."

LATER, IN 1922, IT WAS PUBLISHED IN SIXTEEN LANGUAGES FOR A WORLD-WIDE DISTRIBUTION. IT SOLD OVER A **HALF MILLION** COPIES IN AMERICA ALONE!

ACTUALLY, FORD **RECANTED** IN 1926 WHEN HE WAS THREATENED WITH A LIBEL SUIT.

REALLY?

WHAT DID HE SAY?

HE SAID, IN PART, "...To my great regret I learn that in the 'Dearborn Independent' there appeared articles which induced the Jews to regard me as their enemy promoting antisemitism!"

HE WENT ON TO SAY, "...I am ...mortified that this Journal...is giving currency to 'The Protocols of the Wise Men of Zion,' which I learn to be gross forgeries...I deem it my duty...to make amends for the wrong done to the Jews as fellow men and brothers by asking their forgiveness..."

HE GOES ON BY RECITING SOME OF THE MORE "evil ingredients" in the "Protocols"AND HE REFERS TO IT AS AN "infamous forgery."

DID HIS APOLOGY CHANGE ANYTHING ??

1937
Bern, Switzerland

1945

As the Allies rummaged through documents in the wreckage of defeated Germany, evidence of the influence of the "Protocols" was found by American Intelligence.

HEY, SARGE WHATCHA GOT THERE?

WOW!! **JOSEPH GOEBBELS' PRIVATE DIARIES!** LOOK AT THIS... VOLUME 13...HERE'S A TRANSLATION.

I have devoted exhaustive study to the Protocols of Zion. In the past the objection was always made that they were not suited to present-day propaganda. In reading them now I find that we can use them very well. The Protocols of Zion are as modern today as they were when published the first time! At noon I mentioned this to the Führer. He believed the protocols to be absolutely genuine!

1964
Washington, D.C.

BIG NEWS...THE **UNITED STATES SENATE** HAS ISSUED A REPORT ON THE "PROTOCOLS OF ZION"!

NOT VERY OFTEN DOES CONGRESS DO THIS...

88th Congress } **COMMITTEE PRINT**
2d Session }

PROTOCOLS OF THE ELDERS OF ZION

A Fabricated "Historic" Document

A Report Prepared by the

SUBCOMMITTEE TO INVESTIGATE THE ADMINISTRATION OF THE INTERNAL SECURITY ACT AND OTHER INTERNAL SECURITY LAWS

TO THE

COMMITTEE ON THE JUDICIARY
UNITED STATES SENATE

Printed for the use of the Committee on the Judiciary

U.S. GOVERNMENT PRINTING OFFICE
WASHINGTON : 1964

34-7890

INTRODUCTION

Every age and country has had its share of fabricated "historic" documents which have been foisted on an unsuspecting public for some malign purpose. In the United States such forgeries crop up periodically in the underworld of subpolitics. One of the most notorious and most durable of these is the *Protocols of the Elders of Zion*.

The *Protocols* is one of a number of fraudulent documents that peddle the myth of an "international Jewish conspiracy." In recent years, for example, documents that bear a remarkable resemblance to the *Protocols* have been printed in the Soviet Union as part of the unrelenting campaign against the Jewish minority in the Soviet Union. The one difference is that the documents circulated in the Soviet Union tend to equate "international Jewry" with "international capitalism."

The undersigned Senators have, therefore, recommended the publication of the following analysis by the subcommittee in order to lay to rest any honest question concerning the nature, origin, and significance of this ancient canard.

Essentially, this study is a compendium of a number of separate analyses by authorities in several countries who have had occasion to investigate the origins and circulation of the *Protocols*.

THOMAS J. DODD

KENNETH B. KEATING

1993
California

YES, CAN I HELP?

Los Angeles Times

November 28, 1993

"In what observers called an historic ruling, a Russian court has pronounced the infamous *Protocols of Zion* an anti-Semitic forgery.... [It is] the first such verdict in the land where the fraud originated 90 years ago. 'Up to now, every country has disengaged itself from this shameful book except Russia where it was concocted,' Tancred Golenpolsky, the publisher of the Moscow Jewish newspaper that won the ruling, said Saturday. The court case arose 10 months after Golenpolsky's *Jewish Gazette* accused the radical nationalist Group Pamyat (Memory) of printing anti-Semitic sentiments....Fostering ethnic conflict is punishable under Russian law."

I'M WRITING A GRAPHIC BOOK THAT WILL REVEAL THE TRUE ORIGIN OF THE INFAMOUS "PROTOCOLS OF ZION." I HOPE IT WILL ALERT THOSE WHO ARE IGNORANT OF ITS FALSEHOOD!!

HAW! **GOOD LUCK!** YOU'RE DEALING WITH AN OLD VAMPIRE THAT WILL NOT DIE **IN SPITE OF ALL THE ABSOLUTE PROOF** OF FRAUDULENCE.

RESEARCH

IN **1992**, A **MEXICAN** EDITION OF THE "PROTOCOLS" WAS LISTED IN A FEW CATHOLIC SCHOOLS AS **REQUIRED READING!**

AND THAT SAME YEAR IN **TURKEY**, A NEWSPAPER CARRIED A 40-PAGE INSERT THAT LINKED FREEMASONRY TO JEWISH WORLD POWER **HEADED BY 70 ELDERS!**

AGAIN IN **1992** A **RUSSIAN** EDITION OF THE "PROTOCOLS OF ZION" APPEARED.

WELL, THAT'S THE **WHOLE** STORY, SIR.

THANK YOU! BUT THIS IS **ONLY ONE** ELEMENT OF THE WHOLE STORY!

СИОНСКИЕ ПРОТОКОЛЫ

RESEARCH

1999

2000
Louisiana, U.S.A.

NOT ONLY HERE!! RECENTLY IN **LEBANON,** THE BROTHER OF THE LATE PRESIDENT OF EGYPT, NASSER, PUBLISHED A LEBANESE EDITION OF THE "PROTOCOLS"!

DOWN HERE I DISCOVER THAT "THE CHRISTIAN DEFENSE LEAGUE" IS DISTRIBUTING COPIES OF "THE INTERNATIONAL JEW,"WHICH HENRY FORD PUBLISHED YEARS AGO!

2001
San Diego, U.S.A.

EXCUSE ME WHERE DID YOU GET THIS PAMPHLET?

WHY?

OH! THAT IS PART OF A DEMONSTRATION THIS WEEK HERE AT THE UNIVERSITY BY AN **ETHNIC** STUDENT ASSOCIATION!

WELL, IT URGES THE READING OF THE "PROTOCOLS OF ZION" **FOR THE TRUTH ABOUT THE JEWS.**

EXCUSE ME... YOU'VE GOT A COPY OF THE "PROTOCOLS OF ZION" THERE! ...WHY?

IT REVEALS THE JEWS' PLAN TO RULE US!

THERE'S A **JEW** IN **EVERY** MAJOR GOVERNMENT POST OF THE WESTERN WORLD, SEE?

YEAH!

JEWS ARE BEHIND ALL THE BAD THINGS THAT ARE HAPPENING TODAY!

YEAH, THEIR PLAN IS CLEARLY LAID OUT IN THE "PROTOCOLS," SEE?

WAIT A MINUTE!...WHAT IF IT HAS BEEN **PROVEN** THAT THE BOOK IS A **FAKE?**

IT IS THE INVENTION **OF A FORGER** WORKING FOR THE OLD RUSSIAN SECRET SERVICE IN 1898 TO **DEFAME JEWS**

THE **PROTOCOLS NEVER EXISTED...** NEVER!

2002

FINALLY! HERE'S MY REPORT AND THE MANUSCRIPT THAT NARRATES THE HISTORY OF THE **ORIGIN** OF THIS FRAUD!!

WELL, **NOT YET!**...IN NOVEMBER OF THIS YEAR, A NUMBER OF **ARAB** TELEVISION CHANNELS HAVE BEEN BROADCASTING A TV SERIAL, "KNIGHT WITHOUT A HORSE," BASED ON THE "PROTOCOLS OF ZION"!

IT IS SPONSORED BY THE EGYPTIAN STATE TELEVISION AMONG OTHERS...AND ON NOVEMBER 17, 2001, THE **EGYPTIAN** WEEKLY "ROZ-AL-YOUSSUF" PRAISED THE SERIES FOR **REVEALING THAT THE "PROTOCOLS OF ZION" IS THE CENTRAL LINE** THAT DOMINATES ISRAEL'S POLICY!

OH, MY!

AFTERWORD

by Stephen Eric Bronner

Before his unexpected death at the age of eighty-seven, Will Eisner had a long and distinguished career. He was indisputably one of the American masters of the graphic narrative. His cartoons have a social purpose and yet express a very personal vision. That is surely the case with *The Plot*. Eisner worked on the project, off and on, for over twenty years. It undoubtedly caused him much difficulty. The infamous forgery proclaiming a thinly veiled Jewish world conspiracy, the *Protocols of the Elders of Zion*, has been the subject of heated academic and political controversy since it first burst on the scene. It is easy to understand why the mystery of how this pamphlet was created, no less than the even greater mystery of why it remains so influential, fascinated Will Eisner.

His story is intended for a popular audience. It therefore concentrates on the individuals involved rather than on the complex context in which the fraud was conceived. The backdrop is the sensational Dreyfus affair, in which a Jewish captain on the general staff was falsely accused of selling military secrets to the Germans. From 1894 until 1906, when Alfred Dreyfus was finally pardoned, France was bitterly divided. Liberals and socialists committed to uncovering the real truth and defending "the Jew" battled the aristocratic and reactionary supporters of the military who were unwilling to admit that Dreyfus had been unfairly convicted and that a cover-up had taken place. Things became so difficult for Jews in France that Theodore Herzl, who had been sent to report on the trial of Dreyfus for a Viennese daily, reached the conclusion that a Jewish state offered the only escape from European antisemitism. To that end, in 1897, he convened the first World Zionist Congress.

This was the cultural climate in which the *Protocols* was fabricated. Just as the Dreyfus affair identified Jews with the liberal and socialist forces of modernity, the existence of a Zionist congress provided antisemites with new "evidence" of a Jewish "conspiracy" that needed to be fought and destroyed. The pamphlet made both of these points explicit. It accused Jews of manipulating social reformers and political revolutionaries, the press and the educational establishment, the banks and the labor movements. It insisted that "the Jews" wished to destroy Christian civilization and bring to power their "Elders of Zion." Such wild claims made the *Protocols* extraordinarily useful for reactionaries, who now had a perfect group to blame for the first Russian revolution, which began in 1902 and reached its apex in 1905.

The tract sparked numerous pogroms, organized by feared reactionary groups known as the Black Hundreds, in which thousands of Jews died. As the violence subsided, however, it vanished from public life. But the *Protocols* became popular once again amid the bloody civil war that followed the Bolshevik Revolution of 1917, when the anticommunist "whites" employed it for propaganda purposes against the "reds." Here was the context in which the idea of a "Jewish Bolshevik conspiracy" originally took shape. Only with the defeat of the "whites" would Alfred Rosenberg, the future court "philosopher" of Nazism, import it to Germany along with a copy of the *Protocols* that he had stuffed into his pocket. The man who would serve as the "expert" on race and racial matters started his career by bringing this fabrication to the attention of Hitler and his comrades. Once the Nazis took power, it became what the historian Norman Cohn called a warrant for genocide.

In Europe during the 1920s and 1930s, the *Protocols* was just a bit less popular than the Bible. There is not an antisemitic movement that the pamphlet did not influence. Precisely because the tract was a fabrication, however, its adherents have sought to shroud its origins in mystery. They still try. The authenticity of the work does not seem to matter. But that is because the antisemite, in the great phrase of Jean-Paul Sartre, "turns himself into stone." Bigotry becomes his way of explaining the world without having to justify the explanation through evidence or logic. Antisemitism offers a convenient worldview for all the "losers" who feel themselves threatened by the forces of modernity, who fear the future, and who seek comfort in rigid religious and anti-democratic forms of authority.

Admitting that these traditional forms of authority are becoming increasingly anachronistic would shatter the bigot's sense of self-worth. Better for the losers to find a "scapegoat." And, for different reasons in different circumstances, Jews have usually fit the bill. That is why the *Protocols* will not go away. The pamphlet keeps returning like a bad dream. The need to wake up is what, I know, inspired Will Eisner to produce *The Plot*. It creatively reconstructs the history behind what remains probably the most vicious, and surely the most popular, anti-semitic work ever written. His last original work is a fitting legacy.

References

Because the format of the graphic novel does not easily accommodate the traditional footnote method of documentation, I am using the following references to furnish details for the events represented in this book. Although some of the connecting action between real events has been deduced in order to present a cohesive story, the major narrative is based on reliable sources. Where my research turned up discrepancies, I have chosen to use the facts that appeared more frequently.

Page 8: In the introduction to his translation of *The Dialogue in Hell between Machiavelli and Montesquieu*, John S. Waggoner cautions that "biographical information on Joly is sketchy at best." Henri Rollin's *L'Apocalypse de notre temps* (Paris: Gallimard, 1939), the basis for the *Avant-Propos* to the 1968 edition of the *Dialogue*, is the source most used for material on Joly's life. The year of his birth has been given variously as 1821, 1829, and 1831; there is broader agreement that he died in 1878 and that his death was by suicide.

Page 23: Rachkovsky is described in Norman Cohn's *Warrant for Genocide* as "the sinister and gifted head of the Okhrana [the secret police] outside Russia." He began his career as a minor civil servant. Arrested in 1879 by the internal Russian secret police, he accepted a job in its service rather than go to Siberia. By 1881 he was active in the right-wing Holy Druzhina, which eventually became the Union of the Russian People. Two years later he was adjutant to the head of security service in St. Petersburg. In 1884 he was put in charge of the secret police outside of Russia, and there he remained until 1903. In 1905 he became assistant director of its Department of Police, where he was well known as a skilled plotter and responsible for its huge volume of forged documents. Rachkovsky died in 1911. His involvement in a court intrigue in 1902, his relationship with Sergius Nilus, his militant antisemitic activities, the evidence supplied by Sergei Svatikov and Vladimir Burtsev, and the 1892 antisemitic book *Anarchy and Nihilism*, in which he had a hand—all reinforce the conclusion that he was involved in the creation of the *Protocols of Zion*.

Page 31: Mathieu Golovinski was born in Ivachevka, in the Simbirsk region of Russia, in 1865, according to a report from Paris to the *Washington Times,* November 21, 1899, by Patrick Bishop. Eric Conan, in his article "L'Origine des *Protocoles des sages de Sion*: Les Secrets d'une manipulation antisémite," in *L'Express,* November 24, 1999, states that the Russian historian Mikhail Lepekhine, an authority on the late nineteenth-century publicists, revealed that Golovinski was the forger who authored the *Protocols of Zion.* From the tsar's French files, Lepekhine unearthed the evidence of Golovinski's role. In a 1998 article for *Le Figaro* (France), the writer Victor Loupan reports the Russian historian's findings. Golovinski came from a fading aristocratic family. After the revolution he became an official in the Bolshevik regime. He adopted the title "doctor" and continued to be a prominent figure in the Soviet Union until his death, in 1920.

Page 62: In 1905 Sergius Nilus (1862–1929), with the approval of the Moscow Censorship Committee, published the *Protocols of Zion* as part of the second edition of his book *The Great in the Small.* Later, in 1911, he published a separate edition of the *Protocols.* The mystic Nilus was occasionally invited to the tsar's court. Countess Buturlin, who knew Nilus, recorded an impression of him in a June 1934 statement for the Bern trial. She said that Nilus had three wives, who lived with him and his daughter, that he associated with a group of spiritualist monks, and that he used his daughter as a medium in séances. His *Protocols* enjoyed an enormous success, but he wandered about Russia and continued footloose even after the Bolsheviks came to power. In 1924 and again in 1927 he was briefly imprisoned. On January 14, 1929, he died of heart failure at the age of sixty-six.

Page 69: Philip Graves was a highly regarded correspondent for *The Times* of London, stationed in Constantinople in 1920. In a February 1967 article in *History Today,* Christopher Sykes credits Graves with the recovery of an original French edition of *The Dialogue in Hell,* by Maurice Joly. Graves bought it from a Russian refugee and brought it to England, where he had it authenticated by the British Museum. The article in *The Times* contradicted the *Daily Mail*'s earlier publication of the *Protocols* as the truth.

Page 73: The *Dialogue* used here was translated from the French by Herman Bernstein in his *The Truth about "The Protocols of Zion"* (1935). The *Protocols of Zion* is based on a 1922 translation from the Russian by Victor E. Marsden. Both were edited and supplied for this comparison by Christopher Couch.

Page 98: Hitler was jailed for his role in the Beer Hall Putsch in 1923. The first volume of *Mein Kampf* (My Struggle), which was originally titled *Four and a Half Years of Struggle against Lies, Stupidity, and Cowardice,* was published on July 18, 1925. The second volume, subtitled *The National Socialist Movement,* appeared in 1926.

Page 101: The Bern trial: in 1934, a lawsuit by the Jewish community of Switzer-land was filed against a Swiss Nazi organ, edited by Dr. A. Zander, that pub-lished the *Protocols of Zion*. Dr. J. Dreyfus-Brodsky, Dr. Marcus Cohen, and Dr. Marcus Ehrenpreis represented the plaintiff. The Cantonal Court of Bern found in favor of the plaintiff and fined Dr. Zander on May 19, 1935. His appeal failed in 1937. In August 1934 a court in Grahamstown, South Africa, fined three men $4,500 for publishing a version of the *Protocols*. J. H. Hunt-ing reported these events in a March 1978 article in the *Vineyard*.

Bibliography

Print Publications

Aronsfeld, Caesar C. "The *Protocols* among the Arabs." *Patterns of Prejudice* 9 (July–August 1975): 17–19.

Bach, Hans I. "Projection of the *Protocols*: The Guilt Feeling in Anti-Semitism." *Patterns of Prejudice* 7 (July–August 1973): 24–32.

Bernstein, Herman. *The History of a Lie: The Protocols of the Wise Men of Zion*. New York: J. S. Ogilvie, 1921.

———. *The Truth about "The Protocols of Zion": A Complete Exposure*. New York: Covici, Friede, 1935. Reprint with an introduction by Norman Cohn, New York: Ktav, 1971.

Boym, Svetlana. "Conspiracy Theories and Literary Ethics: Umberto Eco, Danilo Kris and *The Protocols of Zion*." *Comparative Literature* 51, no. 2 (1999): 97–122.

Bronner, Stephen Eric. *A Rumor about the Jews: Reflections on Antisemitism and the* Protocols of the Learned Elders of Zion. New York: St. Martin's Press, 2000.

Cohn, Norman. "The Myth of the Jewish World-Conspiracy: A Case Study in Collective Psychopathology." *Commentary* 41, no. 6 (1966): 35–42.

———. *Warrant for Genocide: The Myth of the Jewish World Conspiracy and the* Protocols of the Elders of Zion. London: Eyre & Spottiswoode, 1967; new ed., London: Serif, 1996.

Conan, Eric. "L'Origine des *Protocoles des sages de Sion*: Les Secrets d'une manipulation antisémite." *L'Express*, November 16, 1999.

Curtiss, John S. *An Appraisal of the* Protocols of Zion. New York: Columbia University Press, 1942.

De Michelis, Cesare G. "Il principe N. D. Zevaxov e i *Protocolli dei savi de Sion in Italia*." *Studi Storici* 37, no. 3 (1996): 747–70.

———. "*Les Protocols des sages de Sion*: Philologie et histoire." *Cahiers du Monde Russe* 38, no. 3 (1997): 263–305.

———. *The Non-existent Manuscript: A Study of the* Protocols of the Sages of Zion. Translated by Richard Newhouse. Lincoln and London: University of Nebraska Press, 2004.

Fox, Frank. "*The Protocols of the Elders of Zion* and the Shadowy World of Elie de Cyon." *East European Jewish Affairs* 27, no. 1 (1997): 3–22.

Goldschlager, Alain. "The Reading of a Hoax or the Endurance of a Myth: *Les Protocoles des sages de Sion*." *Cahiers de Recherche Sociologique* 12 (Spring 1989): 91–101.

Graves, Philip. In *The Times* (London), August 16–18, 1921. [Articles exposing the forgery of the *Protocols*.]

Green, Ronald S. "Scholars Contending with Delusional Ideology: Historians, Antisemitic Lore, and *The Protocols*." *Shofar* 18, no. 2 (2000): 82–100.

Gwyer, John. *Portraits of Mean Men: A Short History of the* Protocols of the Elders of Zion. London: Cobden-Sanderson, 1938.

Hagemeister, Michael. "Wer war Sergej Nilus?: Versuch einer Bio-Bibliographischen Skizze." *Ostkirchliche Studien* 40, no. 1 (1991): 49–63.

Hasian, Marouf, Jr. "Understanding the Power of Conspiratorial Rhetoric: A Case Study of *The Protocols of the Elders of Zion*." *Communication Studies* 48, no. 3 (1997): 195–214.

Hitzig, Michael A. "Russian Court Rules 'Protocols' an Anti-Semitic Forgery." *Los Angeles Times*, November 18, 1993.

Holmes, Colin. "New Light on the 'Protocols of Zion.'" *Patterns of Prejudice* 11, no. 6 (1977): 13–21.

———. "The *Protocols* of 'The Britons.'" *Patterns of Prejudice* 12, no. 6 (1978): 13–18.

Hunting, Joseph H. "The Protocols of the Elders of Zion." *Vineyard*, March 1978.

Joly, Maurice. *Dialogue aux enfers entre Machiavel et Montesquieu*. 1864. Reprint, with a preface by Jean-François Revel. Paris: Calmann-Lévy, 1968.

———. *The Dialogue in Hell between Machiavelli and Montesquieu*. Translated and edited by John S. Waggoner. Lanham, Md.: Lexington Books, 2002.

Korey, William. "The Origins and Development of Soviet Anti-Semitism: An Analysis." *Slavic Review* 31, no. 1 (1972): 111–35.

Ladous, Régis. "*Les Protocoles des sages de Sion*." *Information Historique* 56, no. 1 (1994): 19–23.

Larsson, Göran. *Fact or Fraud?:* The Protocols of the Elders of Zion. San Diego and Jeruslem: AMI-Jeruslem Center for Biblical Studies and Research, 1994.

Lebzelter, Gisela. "The *Protocols* in England." *Wiener Library Bulletin* 31, n.s. nos. 47–48 (1978): 111–17.

Markish, Simon. "Historical and Literary Sources of Russian Antisemitism." *Shvut* 17–18 (1995): 415–23.

Neher-Bernheim, Renée. "Le Best-seller actuel de la littérature d'antisémitisme, *Les Protocoles des sages de Sion*." *Pardés* 8 (1988). Reprinted in Pierre-André Taguieff, *Les Protocoles des sages de Sion*, vol. 2, pp. 367–416. Paris: Berg International, 1992.

Nicault, Catherine. "Le Procès des *Protocoles des sages de Sion*: Une Tentative de riposte juive à l'antisémitisme dans les années 1930." *Vingtième Siècle* 53 (1997): 68–84.

Ribuffo, Leo P. "Henry Ford and *The International Jew*." *American Jewish History* 69, no. 4 (1980): 437–77.

Romano, Sergio. *I falsi protocolli: Il "complotto ebraico" dalla Russia di Nicola II a oggi.* 2d ed. Milan: Edizioni Corbaccio, 1992.

Rowley, David G. "'Redeemer Empire': Russian Millenarianism." *American Historical Review* 104, no. 5 (1999): 1582–602.

Segel, Binjamin W. *A Lie and a Libel: The History of the* Protocols of the Elders of Zion. Translated and edited by Richard S. Levy. Lincoln and London: University of Nebraska Press, 1995. [Segel's book was originally published in 1926 as *Welt-Krieg, Welt-Revolution, Welt-Verschwörung, Welt-Oberregierung.*]

Singerman, Robert. "The American Career of the *Protocols of the Elders of Zion*." *American Jewish History* 69, no. 4 (1980): 437–77.

Smith, David Norman. "The Social Construction of Enemies: Jews and the Representations of Evil." *Sociological Theory* 14, no. 3 (1996): 203–40.

Sykes, Christopher. "The Protocols of the Elders of Zion." *History Today* 17, no. 2 (1967): 81–88.

Targuieff, Pierre-André. *Les Protocoles des sages de Sion.* 2 vols. Paris: Berg International, 1992.

Wilson, Keith M. "The *Protocols of Zion* and the *Morning Post*, 1919–1920." *Patterns of Prejudice* 19, no. 2 (1985): 5–14.

———. "Hail and Farewell?: The Reception in the British Press of the First Publication in English of *The Protocols of Zion*, 1920–1922." *Immigrants and Minorities* 11, no. 2 (1992): 171–86.

Internet Sites

The Anti-Defamation League *http://www.adl.org/*

MEMRI: The Middle East Media Research Institute *http://memri.org/*

The Simon Wiesenthal Center *http://www.wiesenthal.com/*

Beyond the Pale: The History of Jews in Russia
http://www.friends-partners.org/partners/beyond-the-pale/

Acknowledgments

More than any other work involving graphic narration that I have undertaken so far, *The Plot* required an enormous amount of authentication. Dramatizing the creation and history of the *Protocols of the Elders of Zion* needed scholarly help, and I could not have produced this book without the assistance of the following:

Benjamin Herzberg: Early in the writing process, Benjamin provided, from France, a large assemblage of published historical references. This included clues to obtaining an English-language edition of Maurice Joly's book *The Dialogue in Hell*, from which the *Protocols* was plagiarized. A longtime comics collector and fan of the medium, Benjamin understood the mechanics and creative difficulty of undertaking a polemic in sequential art. His selection of the documentation and graphic support was therefore enormously valuable. I thank him and wish him well in his new career at the World Bank.

Christopher N. C. Couch: Soon after I began to frame the narrative sequence, I recognized that I needed a deeper academic support. Upon reviewing my initial "dummy," Chris, a onetime senior editor at Kitchen Sink Press and member of the faculty at the University of Massachusetts, agreed to help me. He translated the French-language edition of Joly's *Dialogue in Hell* into English to provide me with a more reliable document. From this, he assembled a complete page-by-page comparison of *The Dialogue* and each of the twenty-three protocols. For brevity I used only seventeen of the protocols of Marsden's translation of the *Protocols* in this book. I hope to netcast the entire comparison one day soon. Chris also assembled the bibliography herein and secured a collection of essays by scholars. I am grateful to him for providing academic underpinning and historical accuracy during the long year of creative effort.

Ann Eisner: My dear wife, after fifty-four years of encouragement and loving support while enduring my obsessive pursuit of my own profession, set aside some of her own pursuits to help me in the final production. Upon the death of my good brother, Pete, who assisted me during most of his adult life, Ann appeared at the studio, rolled up her sleeves, and said, "How can I help?" It is the first time in our wonderful marriage that we've had a chance to work together on "my work."

Robert Weil: As executive editor of W. W. Norton, Bob read the first, rough dummy of *The Plot* and accepted it for publication. Even before we met, he began to provide me with the really professional editing the book sorely needed. Thanks to his years of experience with major literary works, he transcended my more simple requirement that an editor be the surrogate of the reader. I am grateful for his reinforcement of the premise and argument of this work.

Dave Schreiner: For over twenty years, Dave edited most of my graphic novels. I met him when I affiliated with Denis Kitchen, first my publisher and now, with his partner Judy Hansen, my agent. It was Judy who first shepherded this book up its path to publication. Dave was always dependable and firm, and I relied on his judgment. Indeed, my storage bins contain a number of abandoned book starts regarding which Dave quietly advised, "This is not workable." He read the first draft of *The Plot* and pronounced it "worth your while." I followed his advice. Dave passed away shortly afterward. His soul and spirit is embedded in this work. I hope it will finally meet with his approval.

Index

Will Eisner (1917–2005) was the grand old man of comics. He was present at the birth of the comic-book industry in the 1930s, creating such titles as *Blackhawk* and *Sheena, Queen of the Jungle*. He created *The Spirit* in 1940, syndicating it for twelve years as a unique and innovative sixteen-page Sunday newspaper insert, with a weekly circulation of 5 million copies. As a Pentagon-based warrant officer during World War II, Eisner pioneered the instructional use of comics, continuing to produce them for the U.S. Army under civilian contract into the 1970s, along with educational comics for clients as diverse as General Motors and elementary school children.

In 1978 Eisner created the first "graphic novel," *A Contract With God*, launching a bold new literary genre. Nearly twenty celebrated graphic novels by him have followed. Since 1988 the comic industry's top award for excellence is "The Eisner." Eisner received numerous honors and awards worldwide, including only the second Lifetime Achievement Award bestowed by the National Foundation for Jewish Culture (2002). Michael Chabon's Pulitzer Prize–winning novel *Kavalier and Clay* is based in good part on Eisner.

Expanding on memoir and fiction, *The Plot* represents a new direction for the master storyteller. Utilizing his patented graphic novel format, Eisner unravels the sordid but fascinating history of the twentieth century's most destructive literary hoax.

Umberto Eco was born in 1932 in Alessandria, Italy. He is a professor of semiotics at the University of Bologna, a philosopher, historian, literary critic, and aesthetician. He is the author of the international best-selling novels *The Name of the Rose* and *The Island of the Day Before*, as well as three collections of popular essays: *Travels in Hyperreality*, *Misreadings*, and *How to Travel with a Salmon & Other Essays*. He lives in Milan.

Stephen Eric Bronner is professor of political science and a member of the Graduate Faculties of Comparative Literature and German Studies at Rutgers University. The senior editor of *Logos*, an interdisciplinary internet journal, he has written many books, including *A Rumor about the Jews: Antisemitism, Conspiracy, and the Protocols of Zion* (Oxford University Press) and *Reclaiming the Enlightenment: Toward a Politics of Radical Engagement* (Columbia University Press).